SPRINGBANK
PAPERS

Through the Sun's Eyes
Volume 3

JIM CONLON

Springbank Papers
Through the Sun's Eyes
Volume 3

By Jim Conlon

Published by:
Nicasio Press
Sebastopol, California

ISBN: 979-8-9864100-4-3
Rev. 1

Dedication

To my brother and sister, Bob and Mary, I am forever grateful for the good companionship they have shared with me over the years

Table of Contents

Prologue

I come before you, dear friends, to express my gratitude for my life and the vision so deeply instilled in my soul. Over the years, I have struggled, celebrated, triumphed, and failed.

These reflections were inspired by Pope Francis—by his journey as he embarked on the call of reconciliation, on his five-day visit to Alberta and Quebec in the Dominion of Canada during the summer of 2022. As the shepherd of our lives and the voice of compassion, he continues to venture forth. His enduring presence continues to make all things new.

The words that follow have been inspired by Pope Francis. I share them, as they have left an indelible imprint on my soul.

To Pope John XXIII, who inspired me in my early years, and to Pope Francis now, I give thanks.

I pray that these reflections may contribute to a time of healing and reconciliation for the wounded ones, the Indigenous people of Canada. May they inspire all of us with the living memory of his visit to our country and continue to support each of us as we remember that precious time of Pope Francis in Canada.

SPRINGBANK PAPERS

SPRINGBANK PAPERS

THROUGH THE SUN'S EYES

Dear Pope Francis

You came to Canada to listen and heal our torn and tattered world. You honored and remembered the Indigenous wisdom that is our great gift.

We pray that tomorrow will bring more healing. We pray that we will know, remember, and celebrate our language, our culture, our past.

Today we pray with the Indigenous people, that they may be healed of the abuse and deceptions imposed on them in the past.

We ask for forgiveness as a delegation of pilgrims, as we pray for a new springtime for the people of this great land, that together we may be liberated from past mistakes that caused scandal and shame.

May the bonds of friendship and love be instruments of healing and sparks of fresh, luminous light to celebrate mutual appreciation between our youths and our elders.

May we become a living gift for people of all ages, as together we embark on this sacred journey.

May each of us be empowered to walk onward and upward, to engage in the restoration of our lives and the lives of others, prompted by the legacy of reflections and energized by truth and reconciliation.

May we once more be encouraged with the prospect of living our dreams as we move into the future to fulfill our still-unrealized expectations.

May we awaken to follow the light and transform the darkness of the past and any tendency to sink into sadness and depression.

May each of us become people of freedom, people of the light, givers of the greatest gift we can pass on to enhance each other and our living Earth.

May each person's future call us forward, nourished by the vision of Jesus in the web of life, to provide support for all the days ahead.

As we incarnate a better future, marked by a transition from failure to hope, may we be convinced that we are not alone.

May we join with a like-minded team to keep walking into the future, motivated by vision and practice, as we support each other on our unfolding journey.

Photo: Vatican Media

Walking Together

One important defining moment in the story of Canada was the formation of residential schools.

An unfortunate turn of history brought together a collaboration of government programs and religious communities. Children were taken from their families and compelled to live in a program imposed by governmental and religious authorities. Deep wounds of alienation and cultural isolation were forced on the young people of the Indigenous community. They were deprived of their language and of the ancient wisdom that was the rightful legacy of their elders.

Pope Francis has challenged these practices and supported the elimination of government schools. He addressed the Indigenous people and called his visit a "pilgrimage of penance." He made a sacred commitment to the healing of the cultural genocide and soul trauma that have been inflicted upon the people and their children.

As we move forward, we pray that this healing and restoration may happen.

I give great thanks to the Indigenous ones who were deprived of their sacred legacy of culture, language, and faith.

Today, we are invited to engage in a pilgrimage of reconciliation and forgiveness. We are called to live an authentic life inspired by the resilience of the Indigenous people of Canada, and to provide support and love.

May we join the Indigenous people as they return from the margins of an alienated world and become free of pain.

May we all become a healing presence for every child incarcerated in residential schools. Together with the First

Nation's people, we see the future as a new time of peace, hospitality, and belonging.

As we journey forth, we carry in our hearts the unforgettable stories and sacred exchanges that have been and continue to be the enduring gift of our common journey.

We seek to dissolve the painful memories of cultural genocide as we walk together to transform our world and invoke the restoration of our story.

As we walk into the future together, may our lives be filled with gestures of gratitude and compassion.

May we be guided by a compass of the Good Shepherd as our journey unfolds and we become increasingly aware of what is still possible for us to do.

Guided by an emerging sacred impulse, may we remain immersed in an envelope of joy, love, and fulfillment.

May all things in the future transcend sadness and regret, and may we arrive at a moment of renewed commitment, enthusiasm, and hope.

An Invitation

Ponder what it means to be human.
Create a world beyond war, violence and pain.
Ponder a world of engagement and hope.
Awaken to something entirely new,
a time to make possible a world of beauty
where each human and other-than-human
can flourish and thrive.

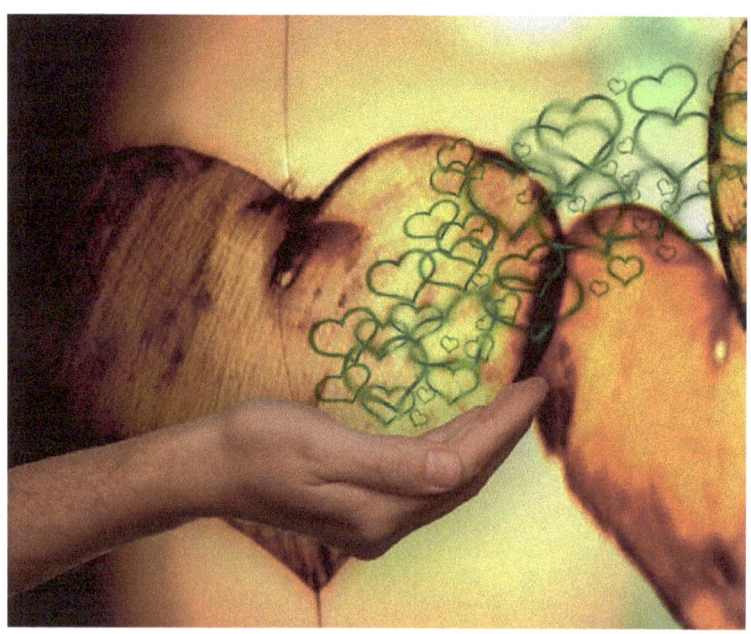

The Ear of Your Heart

Listen with the ear of your heart
to the call of each sacred impulse.
Inspired by your childhood dreams
and challenged by this new age of anxiety,
create the opportunity to make possible
harmony, balance and peace in the days ahead.

The Houses

Come with me.
I want to tell you
about my homes,
the places where I lived.

I was born in Port Lambton,
by the railway tracks.
There my mother made lard sandwiches
for the hoboes
as they passed by on the tracks.

Then there was Eden Villa,
in Courtright, where I lived
with Margaret and Clarice,
for four and a half years.

Also, as a child,
I moved to Sombra
to be with my family.
I lived there until I was on my way
to college and beyond.

In Commemoration

Today we commemorate the life and work of St. John Vianney, the patron saint of parish priests.

I recollect a gathering in Blessed Sacrament Church in London, Canada, around 1970. A good friend joined us, following a meeting with Bishop Emmet Carter. My friend received permission from the bishop to take a leave of absence from the practice of ministry. Later he found employment in Toronto, married, and moved on to a new life.

I recall the stories of good friends I have known throughout the years. One recurring theme comes to mind. Many priests have said to me and others that the best job they ever had was being a parish priest.

As a person whose life has focused on many different programs and positions, I return now to what I view as an eternal truth. We used to say in a colloquial manner, "You hatch them, match them, and dispatch them," meaning "baptize, marry, and bury them."

As I reflect on my journey, especially on this day when we remember the life of St. John Vianney, I give great thanks.

Exultet 2022

On this sacred night, we gather as an Easter people, across the beauty of Springbank and around the world.

Tonight we feel the risen energy, which pulsates of courage and hope for the people of Ukraine and all who suffer violence and discrimination.

May they and all other challenges before us draw on an enduring trust in the hearts of the people who cherish freedom for their homeland and Earth.

Tonight we breathe deeply acts of trust and hope among all planetary people who dare to challenge acts of oppression by those who embrace static dogmas and the domination of people who long for freedom and are energized by the love of country and home.

Tonight we celebrate the onset of a new Easter resurrection moment, with the enduring prayer that peace will flow into the hearts of all those who long for freedom on sacred Earth.

May the killing fields of war be healed at this fresh Easter moment, overflowing into a joyful legacy in yet-unimaginable ways.

On this Easter night, we celebrate the joyful exaltation of existence.

Yes, tonight we celebrate once again the birth of new beginnings.

On this resurrection night, we give great thanks for every cousin and kin risen, new, and truly transformed.

We feel the call today to be resurrection people.

We celebrate and give thanks on this holy night, when we are fully enfolded in the grace of this moment.

Tonight is a new time, everything is fresh and alive.

We are one, infused with a fresh surge of energy, alive, awake.

At this surging cosmic moment, at this hour of the unexpected, on this holy night, I welcome and give thanks for the sound of cosmic music in my heart.

I look back and listen to the passionate presence of our fragile and endangered planet.

On this Easter vigil, may we celebrate the promise and possibility of a new world—wild, wonderful, and beautiful.

We pray tonight that this cosmic Easter energy will heal and transform death and destruction.

On this Easter Exultet night, we gather to pray and joyfully proclaim Christ is risen!

The Cosmic Christ holds all in being, is present in every molecule of existence!

Tonight, as people of song and soul, may we be grateful, may we be Easter people on this holy night.

Alleluia! Christ is risen! The Cosmic Christ is here! Alleluia!

Election Day in America

Does America contradict herself
here at the ballot box today?
Don't corrupt money and abuses of power
threaten a future that is already
uncertain, fragile, failing?
Are we poised to witness
a betrayal of our democratic roots?

Today I exercise my franchise.
Vote for who is best to serve.
Yet I cannot but wonder,
will authentic participation and
informed choice carry the day?
Will democracy survive?

We gather and pray:
May a fresh vision of government
be restored to its original purpose.
May everyone have a voice.
May whatever needs to be done
be our clarion call.

Let us bind up the sores of discontent,
participate in the future
as a united voice of collective wisdom
calling for equity, inclusion, justice,
as each new moment unfurls
out of the womb of abiding peace.

Two Global Prophets

The great guides on our journey into the unfolding future invite us into a deeper sense of mystery.

The legacy and wisdom of Teilhard de Chardin and Thomas Berry are foundational. Teilhard and Thomas were indeed global prophets. Both responded to the challenges of their time with profound wisdom. Their responses to deep questions defined new moments in human-Earth history.

Each possessed a sacramental imagination.

When Teilhard embraced evolution and rejected the ecclesiastical notion of original sin, he was forbidden to publish his theological writings.

Teilhard stated that matter is "the matrix of spirit." For him, matter and spirit were interchangeable realities. Thomas articulated a theology of panentheism and wrote that "the universe is a communion of subjects, not a collection of objects."

Thomas honored the legacy of Teilhard and made these suggestions:

- that we spend more time on creation and less on redemption,
- that we view the human experience as a paragraph in the great cosmic story.

The gifts of Teilhard and Thomas have made significant contributions to human awareness and provided important access to life's deeper mysteries.

Regional Connectors

There is a call within our work to build community and support those with whom we have a common purpose. We call this being a "regional connector." As a regional connector, we provide information, support, and the possibility of common action to others who are energized by their spiritual journey.

Many years ago, I was introduced to the process of developing regional connectors when I met Msgr. Jack Egan at Notre Dame University during a Catholic Committee on Urban Ministry (CCUM) conference. Jack was connected to marginalized people. He realized that they need information, support, and the possibility of common action.

I took what I learned from Jack Egan into my work in Canada and the United States. I realized the wisdom of his approach. When people become regional connectors and reach out to people in their regions, those people are no longer alone and isolated in society. They have a sense of belonging as well as of empowerment.

Lord Acton famously said, "Power tends to corrupt, and absolute power corrupts absolutely." However, if properly administered—and not absolute in nature—power can foster our ability to act. Empowering others provides them with the opportunity to get a handle on a problem and makes it possible for them to act and move forward.

Parallel Times

It was December 10, 1941. A young man, twenty-six years old, rang the doorbell at Our Lady of Gethsemane Abbey in Bardstown, Kentucky. This moment marked the onset of Thomas Merton's monastic journey. World War II had reached a boiling point just three days earlier with the attack on Pearl Harbor. Racism was rampant at the time, as the lack of civil rights continued to wound the souls of people. It was almost twenty years before nine Black students, escorted by federal troops, integrated a high school in Little Rock, Arkansas. And four college students staged a sit-in at a lunch counter in Greensboro, North Carolina, where they were refused service because of the color of their skin.

In many ways, I see parallels with what we are experiencing in 2023. The Russian invasion of Ukraine is boiling, with the possibility of escalating into World War III. The violence of racism remains a deep-seated pathology in the United States. Mass shootings, including racially motivated violence, continue to cause death and devastation. Although ecological issues were not widely known during Merton's lifetime, we can now see their impact, beginning with the Industrial Revolution, on climate change.

We are witness to unprecedented ecological devastation. We understand that Earth is on target to reach key tipping points, many of which most likely are already irreversible.

How do we hold ourselves within this world?

In *When the Trees Say Nothing*, Kathleen Deignen wrote about human sensitivity and care for the natural world. At Springbank Retreat, we focus on what we can do, as a community and on our personal journeys, that demonstrates our care for justice, for Earth, and for her people.

Eucharistic Prayer of the Woods

ALL: We gather today as people of this magnificent planet, alive and alert to the sacred presence of the trees, who call us together this morning. We remember today those who join us on this journey on Earth Mother: sacred trees, the beauty of flowers, each of them and all of us pulsating with the heart of the cosmos.

L: We are alert and awake at this present moment to the wondrous incarnational event that we celebrate this morning with confidence, gratitude, and joy. We are aware of the beauty and brokenness of creation and of those who have preceded us on our journey.

R: This morning, we are invited to immerse ourselves in the wonder of it all. Experience the pulse of the natural world, resonating from within and expressing beauty without boundaries or limits. We sit alert in sacred silence, listening to the quiet and awaiting what is yet to be.

L: Nourished by wisdom and hope, we bask in the beauty of the trees of Earth. It is here, this morning, that we gather at the sunburst of creation and celebrate the divine presence from the cathedral of our soul.

R: Each of us was born into the world, alive with wonder, amazement, and surprise. We discover within each of our hearts a tendency, an invitation, to become uniquely ourselves. Each soul is prompted to embrace the invisible beauty that calls us forth today. As we move to the precipice of new beginnings, we gaze into a yet-unknown future. We seek courage to answer with commitment the call to live into the mystery that sacred spaces, such as the beauty of the verdant woods, call us to.

L: And so we remember the great flaring forth from which hydrogen and helium were born, those amazing supernova moments from which the stars and planets came into existence. Today, in the presence of overwhelming beauty, we celebrate and recall those amazing moments when rocks, life, forests, and consciousness came into existence.

ALL: We celebrate again today the birth of flowers and forests and the coming of Jesus of Nazareth, who now, as the Cosmic Christ, dwells in our hearts and the whole universe. So together we say, "This is my body"—the sign of beauty and brokenness of the Sacred One whose journey we celebrate today.

ALL: Remembering Jesus' total giving of self and his presence everywhere, we raise the cup of celebration, recognizing the Cosmic Christ within all time and space saying, "This is my blood."

R: Alive and wakeful to the beauty of this moment, we recognize what Mechthild of Magdeburg experienced: "God in all things and all things in God." We pause in gratitude and awe at this holy mystery, the source of our life and spiritual nourishment.

The Lord's Prayer: O Cosmic Householder, source of our wisdom, protector, and provider, embracing all that dwells in the heavens, naming all for holiness and justice, in the companionship of empowerment spread throughout the entire creation, as willed by holy wisdom.

In justice, may all be sustained by daily food and relieved of the burden of crippling debts. Lead us not into collusion with any type of violence, and deliver us from all forms of violent oppression. For yours is the empowering desire to radiate on Earth the nonviolent justice of enduring hope.

Tribute to Thomas

If we are to anticipate a flourishing
and vigorous Earth community in the future,
it will be because a man is risen among us
with the wisdom of the prophet Teilhard de Chardin,
the creative spirit of Hildegard,
the compassion of Francis of Assisi,
and the voice of Jesus.
His name is Thomas Berry.
His visionary gift created a movement
that led us to the promised land of the great work,
where we will be transformed
as we create and engage with
the new story that awaits us.

A Pulsating Moment

I feel alive with the presence of the living God,
alive and overflowing into a fresh awareness
that extends to the edges of the cosmos
and simultaneously to the recesses of my soul.
I feel moved in my heart and mind
by this vast moment of grace,
as I ponder the wisdom of life
and all that lies ahead.

Merton's Cosmic Story

Dear Thomas Merton,
you are a healing presence
in this brokenhearted world.
You are my beacon
of wisdom and delight,
a measure of the true self
for which I seek.
Teach me the meaning
of my true self.
Illuminate this moment.
May I become transparent,
open to the wisdom
of your beating heart.

Let Go and Celebrate This Moment

It's a silent day today, still and quiet.
Shelly knows something's happening.
She notices as people pack
and prepare to leave.
Things are different now.

It's time to say goodbye—
which means "God be with you."
"Will I be remembered?" I ask.
"Will others stay in touch?"
As Matthew Fox taught us,
this is my via negativa time.

Goodbye, dear people.
I give thanks to each of you.
Celebrate this precious moment,
this time of love and letting go.
Then begin again.

The Universe Story

The universe story began 13.8 billion years ago. As we discover this story, we discover our origin and evolution in time and are able to view our lives within the context of a cosmic narrative.

Thomas Berry says, "The story of the universe is the story of the emergence of a galactic system in which each new level of expression emerges through the urgency of self-transcendence."

Energized by a sense of the sacred, we celebrate and experience the source of ultimate mystery. We locate our lives within the dynamics of an unfolding, evolving universe. With this in mind, we move forward into the future, with renewed confidence and trust.

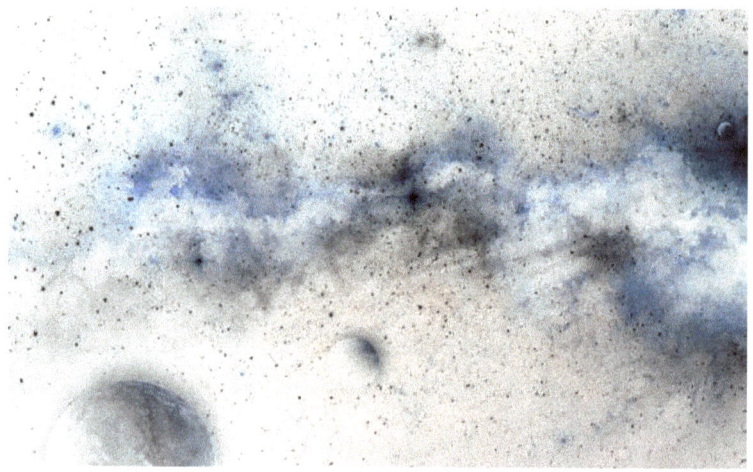

A World of Not-Yet

When the future seems endless
and nothing lies ahead,
I sink into an ocean of wonder.
At this ambiguous moment,
I step back and pray.
As blurred boundaries dissolve
into a world of uncertainty,
I pray for a world of not-yet.

A Wounded Healer

I never thought brokenness could be beautiful. Merton's early days were strewn with chaos, discord, and uncertainty. Early in life, he walked an untrodden path.

Merton was the son of an American mother and a father from New Zealand. Both were artists. By his teenage years, Merton had become an orphan due to the early death of his parents.

Young Merton was talented and gifted but he struggled to make the transition into adulthood. He led an undisciplined life in England. Then he moved to the United States to live under the supervision of his grandfather. He enrolled in Columbia University and received a graduate degree in literature. He taught for some time in New York state. He also worked in Harlem with Catherine Doherty and was deeply moved by her work.

Merton was, in many ways, broken yet beautiful, with a life that was both amazing and fractured. What I most deeply appreciate about Merton and his life's journey is that he became wise and deeply spiritual, even though his path remained unclear.

His was a journey of descent into the depths and ascent into the heights of what is possible. He always desired fulfillment yet constantly seemed willing to settle for less. Some days, his heart leapt with joy, and other days, it was filled with silent emptiness. His heartbeat with the rhythm of the universe, the ache of emptiness, and the expectation of existence. His journey was one of paradox.

The Call to Catholicism

Only recently did I learn that Thomas Merton was inspired to become a Catholic after reading Étienne Gilson's *History of Christian Philosophy in the Middle Ages.* Gilson was well known as a faculty member of the Pontifical Institute for Medieval Studies at Saint Michael's College in Toronto.

This book, which had significance in Merton's conversion, also has personal meaning for me. When I was completing my degree in chemistry at Assumption University of Windsor, I was also pursuing a minor in philosophy. One of the books I was assigned to read in the spring of 1959 was Gilson's book. Little did I know at the time that it had made a significant impact on Merton's decision to become a Catholic.

Many Wells

Thomas Merton was aware and felt a deep connection to the people and spiritual leaders of the East. In 1965, he wrote *The Way of Chuang Tzu*, containing his retranslations of the wisdom of the ancient Taoist sage.

Merton died an untimely death by electrocution in Bangkok, Thailand, following a long-awaited visit to the East. Among his colleagues and friends were the Dalai Lama, Thich Nhat Hanh, and other prophets of the East.

One could say Merton was an architect of deep ecumenism. He understood there are many wells but one river—meaning that many spiritual paths lead to the one underground river that is God, the divine.

Resurgence of Society and Soul

Throughout history—and especially since the Industrial Revolution—the human community has both caused and experienced the onset of events leading to the devastation of Earth. These events have depleted the sources of wisdom throughout the world.

However, I also believe that the resurgent spirit of Earth and its peoples has begun to emerge. I see a deep-seated psychic power beginning to assert itself. This fresh emergent energy springs from a transgenetic impulse and provides us with vision, energy, and practice. It can liberate us and the planet from the forces of confinement that have opposed the unfolding of society and soul.

Merton and the Meaning of Sacrifice

Have you ever wondered about the meaning of sacrifice in your life and in that of Thomas Merton?

On one level, sacrifice simply means to make holy. Rabbi Abraham Heschel said, "Just to be is holy." Meister Eckhart said, "Is-ness is God."

I recall a story from the Old Testament about Abraham and Isaac. As the story goes, at first, Abraham thought he must surrender his son, Isaac; because God demanded it, he must let go of his attachment to his son.

However as the story unfolds, God renders a choice that makes sacrificing Isaac no longer necessary. Abraham's son is freed.

Over the years, this story has made an indelible impression on me. "Sacrificing our Isaacs" is an important moment in each of our spiritual journeys. We reflect on this story as we ponder the significance of sacrifice for our spiritual journey.

An Enduring Promise

Each day, cable news belches out views of violence around the country. On this past July 4th, it was at a parade in the primarily Jewish community of Highland Park, Illinois. Shortly before that, it was in a classroom in the Latino community of Uvalde, Texas. And before that, it was in a shopping mall frequented by the African American community in Buffalo, New York.

At the same time, we hear daily reports from war-torn Ukraine, as people draw their last breaths while fighting for the freedom of their country.

How can we respond to this devastating barrage of news?

Our thoughts and prayers will not stop the next mass shooting or the next world war.

But we can each take concrete action to build a world of greater promise, to provide information, support, and the possibility of common action in the days ahead.

Like blades of grass fighting for life in a dying soil, we can unite with others to work for a brighter tomorrow. We can find others who are similarly convinced and prayerfully resolved, and together work to make a difference that will be felt by the world around us. This work can be our enduring promise, our gift to future generations.

Gather and Celebrate

The ever-present symbols
flow across my paper,
blending every tint and nuance.

May the static and the evolving
come and wander here.
Rest, then wander, then rest again.

May we gather and celebrate
in this mixing, mingling moment,
here among the trees.

My Gospel View

In my gospel view, I strive to create a synthesis of the three dynamic principles of the universe: differentiation (nothing is the same), interiority (within-ness and subjectivity), and communion (everything is inter-connected).

This trinitarian dynamic reflects the divine presence in the world. Differentiation is a reflection of the creator God. Interiority is a reflection of the son of God. And communion is a reflection of the Holy Spirit. With this in mind, the three dynamic principles not only have implications for justice and beauty in the world but also reflect the heart of the divine.

Our challenge is to put this vision into practice. As we do that, we become what Paulo Freire called "a vagabond of the obvious." He was referring to his travels throughout the world, during which he strove to join theory and practice, to shed light on what should be obvious in our perception of reality, to bring an awakened awareness to daily experience.

Awareness of the world around us also calls us to become what Saul David Alinsky named a "therapist of the apathetic." Through our practice of deep listening and recognition, we pay attention and listen with the ear of our heart.

The Dynamic Principles of the Universe

Thomas Berry wrote about the three dynamic principles: differentiation, subjectivity, and communion.

These three tendencies are arrived at through empirical observation. They require no mathematical formulae or research. I discovered through reflecting on these principles that they can be applied in all dimensions of our lives and our culture. They are self-evident and essential to achieve an understanding and practice of creating a world replete with values and beauty.

As we sense ourselves enveloped in an unfolding future, we return to a deepening awareness of these dynamic principles of the cosmos. They are our guides as we explore an operative future for our lives.

Differentiation shows us that nothing in creation is the same. This amazing awareness brings us to the conclusion that the divine does not repeat herself. Every snowflake, every leaf on a tree, every forest, every friend is not the same.

Isn't it amazing that nothing in the universe is the same as anything else? No two puppies, no two people, neither you nor I are identical to others. As a result, each of us is called to celebrate and honor the uniqueness present in creation. We are invited into an awareness of amazement that God does not repeat herself. Our challenge is not to imitate others but to be uniquely ourselves.

Another way of saying this is that every creation is always in the beginning, always on the verge of being born. Meister Eckhart said in response to the question "What does God do all day?" that God lies on her maternity bed giving birth. If everything is new and unique, we can conclude that God is the youngest among us, always engaged in a process of beginning.

It is paradoxically true that each experience of creativity that is fresh and about to be born is not only unique but also in communion with everything else. Here, we exalt and celebrate the wisdom that is separate, distinct, and in deep connection with all things in the universe, which we now perceive as one.

We sense and celebrate the realization that, together in the universe, we are moving toward a focus on oneness. From this perspective, we can say that nothing in the universe is fractured, separate, or fragmented from something else.

Not only is everything in the universe unique, but at the same time, it is also one. Together, we are empowered to make this our prayer. May we be one. May we be holy. Make us one again.

We live at the turning point of profound wisdom and truth. We are all in communion with what is, replete with both uniqueness and interconnectedness. This is the sacred paradox of our universe story journey.

This is a profound mystery flowing out of our experience of creation. From within this deep, living dynamic, we are called to blossom forth, to give expression to a living truth— to a living memory that is both distinct from and interconnected with all that is.

Now is the time to awaken to this holy mystery. It is a revelation that reveals both communion and difference in all of the cosmos and creation.

We remain grateful for this paradoxical dynamic that is formed and focused in all our experiences.

A third dimension also present in all of our lives is the sense of a deep withinness, a subjectivity that lingers and resides in the interiority of the soul. It provides a focus for the deep wells of wisdom that give expression to the unimaginative depths of the imagination.

This significant insight is found in the heart of the universe and each of our lives. It is expressed in a profound realization that is beyond all understanding. As we continue to explore, it unfolds into a sense of nothingness, an amazing felt sense of emptiness, a sacred abyss.

As we move forward, we transcend this current moment and reflect on the sacred mystery of the universe that lies beyond conscious thought. Yet at the same time, this deep mystery embodies and gives expression to withinness and interiority.

The Transmission of Values

One of the most profound moments in my search to bring beauty to the world is the gift I now understand as the transmission of values, which was named by geologian Thomas Berry. This gift finds expression in his writings and provides an understanding of how to achieve a world of beauty and belonging in society and on Earth.

The transmission of values has become central to the vision and practice of my work. I arrived at this awareness by examining the three dynamic tendencies that are available to us in all of life. My thoughts on the transmission of values also reflect deeply held intuitions from my personal background as well as early understandings I gained from Saul Alinsky in the field of community organization and from the approach to popular education (conscientization) Paolo Frere described in *Pedagogy of the Oppressed*.

The three dynamic principles of the universe are both empirical and capable of being translated into cultural form. Through our reflections, we make possible the experience and expression of the presence of divinity in cultural form in society.

We search for an expression of the values that are included and practiced in our spiritual journey. Through this exploration, we realize that the three tendencies give meaning, purpose, and value to our journey.

In and through the inculturation of these principles, we are able to translate and make possible the wisdom and wonder of the dynamics of the universe and Earth. We could say that the relationship between subjectivity, inter-connectedness, and uniqueness create the ground for a comprehensive context for ecological, social, and personal expression in cultural form.

Each of us is genetically encoded for the society into which we were born. However, in this postindustrial age, we are profoundly influenced by the dominant culture, which continues to divide and destroy the wisdom and beauty that would be possible if we were to create a society out of the values of these principles. Our challenge today is to return to a world of beauty and imagination, as we widen our awareness of these three principles.

As we give expression to this creative process, we both observe and participate. We gather to give thanks for the enduring gifts of beauty, trust, and gratitude for all we have received. We celebrate these principles as a vehicle for the transmission of values, and we experience inter-connectedness as they overflow into the generativity of all through the manifestation of beauty, wonder, and belonging.

Our soul work here at Springbank is nothing less than living at the cusp of new beginnings. May our sabbatical time invite us to participate in the delivery room of our soul work.

Our Next Chapter

As we venture forth
into the next chapter of our journey,
we explore how to make manifest
an experience of beauty.

We commune with sacred Earth,
dedicate our lives
to becoming a healing balm
for our planetary soul.

We allow ourselves to be bathed
in the radical energy of creation,
aware that each and every creature
is a book about God.

The Call

We feel a call echoing
the wisdom of Meister Eckhart
to enact whatever needs to be done,
to embrace sacred mystery
and to carry out the vision of global prophecy
embodied in the hearts and minds
of Teilhard and Thomas.

We listen to the promptings of our heart
and to the needs of Earth
as we prepare for our great work in the days ahead.
We listen to each sacred impulse
that prompts us to acts of compassion
through the expression of
harmony, balance and peace.

I Walk in Beauty

I grew up in Ontario, Canada, where we learned about the Chippewa and Potawatomi tribes of southwestern Ontario and Michigan. I was deeply influenced by what I learned about their Indigenous cultures.

Today, through clay, color, and word, we at Springbank continue to discover how art, poetry, music, and ritual emerge into our awareness.

I recall a ritual I used to participate in at Holy Names University, when I was living in California. We performed a circular dance while we chanted a Navaho prayer that had been translated into English by the poet laureate Ted Hughes:

> I walk in beauty before me.
> I walk in beauty behind me.
> I walk in beauty above me.
> I walk in beauty below me.
> I walk in beauty all around me.
> The whole world is beautiful.
> The whole world is beautiful.
> The whole world is beautiful.

Meeting Thomas Berry

Thomas Berry was a man of towering stature and a compassionate heart.

One day, while visiting my sister in Springlake Heights, on the New Jersey shore, I ventured forth on a train to New York. My plan for the day was to visit Thomas Berry at his residence at the Riverdale Center for Religious Research.

When I arrived, I was cordially welcomed by Thomas and Brother Conrad. We had lunch together, followed by a good conversation. I stayed over night and had a restful sleep.

The next day, Thomas introduced me to the library that housed his current work. We were surrounded by many shelves containing unpublished work from his time at Riverdale Center. He selected several essays and offered me a bundle of unpublished writings to bring back to New Jersey.

Thomas took me to the subway, and I boarded a train back to New Jersey. I was filled with gratitude for our visit.

Foremost among my reflections on the train was appreciation for the contribution of Teilhard de Chardin, the Jesuit priest who influenced Thomas's work. Teilhard and Thomas brought a hopeful and optimistic message to the country and the culture. Both refused to turn away from the horrors of suffering and war; yet, at the same time, they remained people of the resurection, whose visions were nourished by a spirituality founded on the reality of a creative yet unfinished universe.

They wanted people to see the challenges of beauty, wonder, and belonging as we wander between two worlds: the love of God and the love of Earth. We experience our love of God in and through the Earth. This vision was a great healing paradox. Together, Teilhard and Thomas transformed what was a static dogma into an unfolding evolutionary view.

Thomas transformed a fourteen-billon year history into a vital and vibrant healing vision. He proclaimed to the world the vision of the universe story and reminded us that we need to spend more time with the beauty and wonder of the natural world.

When Thomas left us in 2009, his passing became a supernova moment for people studying his work. I attended his funeral in Green Mountain Monastery, and a subsequent tribute at the Cathedral of the Divine in New York City. I gave thanks then, as I do now, to Thomas for his contribution to healing the damage caused by the postindustrial era to the planet and to all beings.

Sunshine

Sunshine warms each day,
invigorates my soul.
Sunshine lifts my spirit,
illuminates our land.

I awake to each new day
full of promise, sunshine and care.
Sunshine celebrates
the freshness of each day.

Each sunbeam glows
to dispel the dark,
cascades into wonder
in the springtime of my soul.

A Cosmic Shift

Perhaps the great challenge for us today is to reflect on the signs of the times and proceed in a way to show we appreciate what God is "up to" in our midst.

To experience this cosmic shift requires that we believe differently (that is, learn to trust) and act differently (that is, learn to engage) as we welcome the unfolding presence of the spirit.

Through this energetic vision, here at the crossroads of time and eternity, we embrace what has gone before and invite a new and dynamic integration of science, art, and mysticism.

The inclusion of cosmology through the integration of science, art, and mysticism makes possible the presence of fresh energy and a zest for life. When this inclusion is lacking, there also is a lack of energy, vision, and wisdom. Something is no longer present. In my view, reflections on our story enable us to consider our origins, our present moment, and our glimpse of the future.

In this way, we can move forward in anticipation of our uncertain future and are able to knock at the door of tomorrow.

Ash Wednesday: Springtime in My Soul

In our tradition, we celebrate the beginning of Lent as Ash Wednesday. Another word for Lent is spring. The poet Rilke writes, "It's spring again. The earth is like a child that knows poems by heart."

One metaphor for Lent is spring cleaning. It is a time when your home sparkles with radiance and a fresh sense of newness. We prepare ourselves with acts of love shown to all living beings. It's a spring cleaning of our souls.

While we celebrate these sacred moments of Easter, we are also reminded of the reality of death on this Ash Wednesday. As we give and receive ashes and are blessed, we pray that we may see the transformation of ashes across Ukraine. We pray for these brave people, that they and all the peoples of the world may find the blessings of peace.

Thank You

The Santa Claus parade
and Black Friday shopping
threaten us with promises
of a more-is-better life.

All around us,
the dominant culture
plunges us into a world
of money, power and greed.

O dear friends,
for a happy Thanksgiving,
may a simple and heartfelt
"thank you" suffice.

A Cosmic Prayer

God of the cosmos,
source of love and life,
be with me now.
Breathe fresh energy
into the heartbeat of this day.

In my search for meaning
and wisdom,
be with me now.
Heal my brokenness,
knit together a poultice
for this fractured soul.

As the sun rises
on this dark and dusky morning,
be with me now.
Suffuse my soul
with the beauty of this day.

I Need to Pray

Pardon me now. I need to pray.
Standing with the beauty
of all creation, unfolding
within and all around,
today I need to pray.
I pray in gratitude
for the wondrous stories
to be told in every minute of the day.
I feel bombarded with beauty,
a nourishing banquet prepared
at the table of new life.
On this Thanksgiving Day,
I need to pray.
For all that is, I say Thanks.
And for all that will be, I say Amen.

Gratitude, Anger and Hope

A message came to me this morning,
simple, sacred and brief.
A fresh message of gratitude and grace.
"Happy Thanksgiving," I whisper
and then begin to pray.

Memories of what we have done
to each other and to the land
tumble into my awareness.
I remember the massacres
of Indigenous people.

As we give thanks
for the abundance of Earth
that has nourished our bodies
and strengthened our souls,
let us also honor the First Nations people,
who first called this land their home.

Christmas 2022

Merry Christmas, dear friend!
Meister Eckhart reminds us
that we must not only
celebrate and remember
the birth of Christ 2000 years ago
but we must also recall,
in this incarnational moment,
that now is the time
when Christ is born today among us.

Yes! This is the time to welcome
the birth of Christ in 2022,
as we celebrate
the Cosmic Christ's presence
in the midst of our prayers,
beauty and hope.

On this Christmas day,
may this cosmic wisdom
dispel all darkness and fragments of war.
May this Christmas day be a time
when the mystic and prophet in each of us
flourishes and becomes fully alive.

On this Christmas day,
we pray that the radiant true self in each of us
becomes a vibrant presence
alive throughout this sacred Earth
and all creation.

May each of us
on this Christmas 2022,
recognize and give great thanks
for the precious gifts we have received,
as gratefulness flows
across the world.

The Flesh Became Word

Teilhard gave the believing community the gift of evolutionary faith. Part of this gift was a profound incarnational insight.

For Teilhard, "the flesh became word." With this belief, he put to rest the dualism that often differentiates matter and spirit. There is no separation between the presence of divinity and what he referred to as his "divine milieu."

When we can say with Teilhard that the flesh became word, we celebrate the reality that all matter is soaked in God. We affirm that God is present in secular experience. Every molecule of matter is fully infused with divinity. This is a manifestation of profound mystery.

We witness and experience this great mystery as it continues to unfold.

Just as a child and parent experience interchangeable realities, so too can we both say that the word became flesh and also that the flesh became word. Both are true.

Our experience of this deep mystery has become our operative theology. It is a sacred moment in which we discover the wisdom that bubbles out of the recesses of our minds and hearts. When we declare the total integration of God's presence, we are able to shift our worldview so it is no longer static and we are no longer stuck in a world of separation.

Pulsation

Walk among the trees.
Listen to Hildegard.
Experience the inhalation
and exaltation of existence.
As the healing heart of the cosmos
pulsates across the far-off sky,
listen deeply
as the trees say nothing.

Pilgrims of Divine Care

Today we have entered a new territory in cultural identity for the Indigenous people of Canada.

May we join with the Indigenous family of pilgrims.

The lives of both youth and elders remind us that we are all pilgrims of divine care.

We join with St. Kateri Tekakwitha as the feminine soul of our nation. Her life provides a holy recollection of wisdom and gratitude. We pray that this wisdom and gratitude will continue into the future.

Known among your people as Lily of the Mohawks, we join you to pray for reconciliation and peace and gratitude.

We honor the wisdom and gifts of Indigenous people, among them Nicholas Black Elk, leader and catechist, whose name has been put forward for canonization. We await the time when he will be proclaimed a saint.

As we celebrate the Indigenous wisdom of the people of Canada, we are called to create a dynamic integration of religion and culture, as expressed through language, dance, and music.

Sacred Place

Do you feel it now?
You have arrived
at the doorway of new beginnings.
Everything you dare to hope for
is possible. Nothing is impossible.
At this cosmic moment,
you feel a splash of wonder
gurgle in your mind and heart.
You have arrived in this sacred place,
where you belong.

A Christmas Moment

Shelly and I went for a walk
on this cold sunlit morning.
Memories tumbled into thought.
When I was a child,
we would carefully place
an apple and cookies
underneath the Christmas tree.
It was our gift to Santa Claus,
for when he stopped by
in the night to bring us gifts.

Then one day I read an article
in the *Windsor Daily Star*
about parent propaganda.
I was sorely disappointed.
A question arose in my heart:
What does Christmas mean anyway,
if it's not about Santa Claus
and the chimney?

Now I continue to ask,
Is Christmas not about plunging
into a time of new beginnings?
Isn't it about falling in love
with the surprise of a December morn?
About falling into a fresh awareness
of generosity and of God,

falling so we are open
to a wondrous day of gratitude,
when all creation and every soul
is fresh, young and new?

The Historical Jesus and the Cosmic Christ

One evening when I was driving Thomas Berry back to his motel following the presentation he had made to students at Holy Names University, I posed a question that had been on the minds of our students over the years: "How do you understand the relationship between the historical Jesus and the Cosmic Christ?"

His answer was simple and profound: "When a child gazes at their mother, they see the most intimate and personal relationship they will ever know. At the same time, the child's mother represents the most cosmic experience the child will ever know."

His words healed any trace of the kind of dualism, or separation, that is often encountered by people of faith. Thus he made possible an encounter that is both cosmic and deeply personal. Each of us has received an integral gift from his words.

Surrender

When we ponder the depths of our experience revealed in the via negativa, the second path of creation spirituality, it becomes possible to surrender and let go and let be.

Out of emptiness and profound surrender, we are able to let go of pain and become immersed in what lies ahead.

To celebrate and experience deep wisdom provides a basis for an expansive imagination that overflows into wondrous splashes of creativity, wild moments that become resurrection events.

It is from here that we are able to celebrate a springtime in our soul. Our brokenness is healed, and the ethos of our soul is renewed and restored.

Life

Life is an adventure,
a challenge, an invitation.
A cosmic dance
between joy and sorrow.
An invitation into cosmogenesis.
A dance into rivers of grace.
Those who love, know this.
May we become grateful.
May we become one.
Make us joyful again.

To Awaken

Today I return to a conviction long held.
I believe the challenge of this day
is to awaken my creative imagination,
to make breakthrough possible.

I pray for a wondrous new beginning,
a chance to muster my remaining energy.
I pray for the deep wound of separation
to be healed and to be brought back to health.

From the Tunnel to the Green Door Revisited

In 2018, I responded to an invitation from Sr. Brigid Lawlor, with the Sisters of Charity of the Good Shepherd in France. The invitation was to join a team of women and men to assist in the preparation of some forty sisters who were preparing for final vows in their community.

The name of the project and the focus of their work was to be known as the Tunnel and the Green Door. The title was a metaphor for their spiritual journey.

The tunnel, founded on the geography of the mother house of the Sisters of Charity, represented the constriction and struggle with obstacles that predictably show up on their journey to final vows.

The green door is a symbol for the promise and possibility of freedom. It represents a doorway to self-expression. The sisters are presented with opportunities for liberation as they prepare for and celebrate the final vows of their religious life.

Today, I understand the tunnel and the green door as an avenue and doorway into a new time of freedom and fulfillment as we move forward in our lives to accomplish our great work and life's purpose. It is the destiny that each of us are called upon to realize.

Merton's Doorway

The words that erupted from Merton's soul
evoked a passion to give expression
to the hidden mystery pulsating within me.
His words hovered in my mind and heart,
creating a passage to newness and new life,
a doorway into beyondness.
I felt a prompting, an invitation,
to compose words not fully understood
yet purposeful for my journey.

The Thomas Berry Book Room

Here in the hermitage at Springbank, I look around the book room and feel surrounded by friends. In the silence of the morning, I glance at the titles and feel embraced by the memories of each author and their words.

The books on these shelves are my friends because they tell the story of my journey. They tell the stories of many others as well.

Over the years, I've read many of these books as I searched for the guidance to be gleaned from the authors' participation in the great work of our time.

In the book room, I am filled with gratitude and admiration. I give thanks for the wisdom of the prophetic voices who dared to guide our lives into hopeful transformational moments. I feel inspired to take up the challenges they left with us here in the Thomas Berry book room at Springbank Retreat.

Our Quest

We seek a way to creatively
see, dance, proclaim
and shiver into an awareness
of what it means to be human.
Each of us is called to express,
celebrate and ponder
what is bubbling up in our souls.
We seek to be born again
with new words, new language,
an incarnational vision that is fully alive.
We venture forth out of the darkness
and into the orbit of a guiding star,
twinkling in our imagination and the cosmos,
as we wonder and wait to be born again
and to experience the moment, the quest,
that summons us into life.

Anniversary Celebration

We gather today to give thanks and celebrate the twenty-seventh anniversary of Tommy and Cheryl's special moment, when they became husband and wife. Today we recall the precious moments when each was born and entered into a life of new beginnings. It was a time of joyful awakening when, from the very beginning, they experienced a life of joy, gratitude, and profound expectation. With each passing day, now twenty-seven years later, we remember and give thanks for the time that has passed and for new beginnings.

When we feel immersed in the holy mystery of love that brought Tommy and Cheryl together, we are reminded of the depths of friendship and bonds of love that continue to deepen and unfold in each of our lives on this grateful Sunday. We express gratitude for this special moment and are filled with joyful anticipation for the days ahead.

Happy Birthday, Dad

Today is August 25, 2022. It is the anniversary of the day when Richard Conlon was born.

His father was Thomas Conlon, and his mother was Mary Doran. He was one of five brothers: Gus, Fred, Leo, and John. And two sisters: Mary and Nell.

His mother went on to eternal life when he was but a child. In many ways, he was cared for by his older sister, Nell.

He left school at grade six to work on the family farm. In later years, he spent the winters in the Windsor/Detroit area working in the automotive industry.

He met the woman who was to be his wife, Elizabeth Bedard, in Port Lambton, Canada. Elizabeth was the daughter of Alexander Bedard and Olive Gravelle. Together, Richard and Elizabeth gave birth to three children: Mary Olive, Robert Joseph, and James Alexander.

My father, Richard, was a fine and respected man in his community. As an employee of the Department of Highways of Ontario, he rose to the position of foreman and cared for the highways in summer and winter. He supervised the snowplowing and protected the safety of drivers.

However, his position of leadership was terminated when the Progressive Conservative Party of Ontario was elected in the 1930s. As a result of losing his position and in order to receive a future modest pension, he lied about his age and began work for the Pierre Marquette railway company. He eventually retired with a modest pension in the early 1970s.

He often attended baseball games to watch Bob and Jim play.

In his later years, after his family had been raised, he lived alone in the family home. His wife had died when she was about sixty years of age.

He enjoyed visits with his neighbors. He often invited them to his front porch to share a story.

Today, I join my brother Bob to share and express a joyful happy birthday to Richard Conlon. Happy Birthday, Dad.

Sunday in Sarnia

It was Sunday afternoon
at Our Lady of Mercy church in Sarnia.
Tom McKillop, a priest from Toronto,
the director of Youth Corps,
was headed to the parking lot,
on his way home,
after concluding the weekend program.
It had been about Auschwitz
and the devastation caused by war,
including the dissolution of human dignity
and the casting aside of basic respect.
As I stood there on that Sunday
watching Tom walk away,
I felt as if each of my days
had been punctuated by a series of aneurysms.
Nothing remained the same.

Aspiration

We listen in silence
to the voice of God.
We make our prayer today,
enveloped by the gaze of Jesus.
We give thanks in joyful recollection
of times long past,
moments when we were grateful
and found God in soup kitchens, prisons.
The words of Meister Eckhart
echo in my heart:
"Where there is Isness, there God is."

Ode to Poetry

Poets are voices from another world.
They speak the language
of sound, smell, taste and silence.
Their words ripple across
the landscape of my soul.
I dive deeply into other modes
of understanding, then listen,
let my heart speak poetry,
my imagination sing.

Cosmic Creativity

Today we embark
on an adventure of cosmic creativity.
Immersed in the holy mystery
and radical amazement,
it is an adventure
that is deeply personal and vastly cosmic.
We engage in this discovery
of the true self
within the context
of an expanding universe.

Gratitude Today

Here I am, Lord, waiting in the night,
waiting for I know not what.

Thank you for days long past,
and especially for what awaits.
Each day is a special gift.
Each promises one more tomorrow.

I say thank you once again
for each day gone by.
And if I may be so bold as to say,
thank you for what is yet to be.

Perhaps gratitude is
our most honest prayer.
A breath of thanks is
our most ardent wish.

O Lord, one breath of gratitude
carries me through the long night.

Hunger

There's a hunger in my heart
that wants to live,
to awaken to what
is still possible for me to do,
to write, to walk, to pray.

With each passing day,
I arrive at a new cosmic moment,
a moment that promises
to transport me in my quest,
to recapture new beginnings,
and challenges me to respond.

What awaits me now
is to sink into life's purpose,
continue on and discover what's next
as the days tick by,
and today transforms into tomorrow.

Turning Point

We are at a turning point
in human-Earth history.
It is a time in the vast wonder of the universe,
when prompted by the stirring in our souls,
we join with good companions
to imagine and make possible
a world of beauty, sacredness and depth.

Together we take up the task
to heal what is broken
and renew the face of the Earth
and cross the threshold of destiny,
to make possible
a world of beauty, wonder and belonging.

A Hope-Filled World

I wish to live in a world where
being alive is a gift,
where resolve and purpose rule each day.
I wish to live in a world, a hope-filled world,
where every tree and branch
shivers with ecstasy and beauty.
I wish to live in a world
where the elderly are cherished
and the little ones revered.
I wish to live in a world
where stories are told,
where tomorrow matters and
yesterdays become a treasure of the past.
I wish to live in a world
where the future holds possibility.
This is the world in which I want to live.

The Waters of Life

Poet Sophia de Mello Breyner Andresen wrote, "I'm listening yet I do not know if what I hear is silence or God."

I am listening, and I hear a voice. It says, "Cast yourself on the waters of life."

Today each of you is at the precipice of new beginnings.

We remember today those who have gone on ahead: all saints and all souls.

These friends of God and the prophets invite each of us to compose a new chapter on our journey. It is a time to fearlessly proclaim, here at the crossroads, that we are no longer confined by the guidance of the past.

We celebrate the new vows that await us, the fresh sacred promises of patience, ambiguity, and risk.

With patience, we move forward, aware that tomorrow we will be required to make powerful changes, to engage in a prolonged effort to work on what is yet to be accomplished.

With risk, we prepare to launch into each new tomorrow, without clarity about how things will turn out. As we embrace each not-yet in our lives, we become confident as we wonder how tomorrow will turn out.

With ambiguity, we call forth the fresh capacity to both wait for and leap into the future.

With this in mind, we move forward, immersed in a compassionate mind and empowered by a thinking heart. We go out and promise faith in an unknown future.

Now is the time to reinvent our lives and renew the face of Earth. Today, we become people empowered and engaged in a hope-filled future.

We are positioned on the cusp as we discover the fire of the cosmos in our hearts and realize the person we are called to be.

Nakedness and God

I want to heal your presence, my friend,
feel the absence of what I cannot see,
celebrate your essential beauty
and the silent wisdom of your soul.
I feel an anxious longing
to hear the beating of your heart,
to touch the naked longing of your soul.
This longing is an intersection
of nothingness and God.
I am alone today, separate yet united,
in the nakedness of God.

Finding Spiritual Guidance

Traditionally, one begins the spiritual journey with a companion who serves as a guide using the practices of listening, reflection, and recognition. This is a journey without the intrusion of advice, analysis, or interpretation. Spiritual companionship need not follow a strictly human-centered approach; it can be experienced in new and different ways.

At Springbank, we have learned that spiritual guidance can be accessed in non-anthropocentric ways. For example, our dogs Max, Jake, Shelly, and Bennie provide wisdom and guidance in ways that we are perhaps still trying to understand.

We may also choose to be guided by the particular characteristics of the world around us. Some would call this *Sitz im Leben*, meaning in the context in which we live. In this way, we receive guidance and focus for our journey from dawn to dusk each day, and through the four seasons of the year. We also pay attention to the climate that is operative in the bio-region where we live as well as to the social and cultural context in which we live.

Thoughts on Creativity

You can't do spirituality without art.
Spirituality resides more in the imagination
than in the intellect.
Resurrection is the theological word for creativity.
Meister Eckhart asks, "What does God do all day?"
And he answers, "From all eternity,
God lies on a maternity bed giving birth."
Our greatest act of creativity is to create ourselves,
to be true to our own uniqueness.
We can never become a model,
nor can we model our life
after that of any other person.

A Great Unfolding

The great story unfolds.
We are in the world.
each alive with wonder,
amazement and surprise.
Each new day we discover
within our hidden hearts
an invitation to become
our unique self.
Today we dare to knock
on the doorway of what is possible.

We live in the dynamic
unfolding cosmos.
Each day we embark
on a search for meaning
and purpose.
Moment by moment,
we become astonished
as each evolutionary instant
announces the transformation
of consciousness.

We peer over
the vast orchard of possibility
that awaits us.
We dare to grow our soul
and savor and express
a profound hope
at this turning point
on our unfolding journey.

God of Wisdom

Source of love and light,
be with us now.
Guide our hearts and minds
as we listen to
the influence of your spirit.

May we be prompted
to bring peace and healing
to this sacred place
as we open ourselves
to the joys and sorrows of life.

Today we pray,
may we be hopeful,
may we be grateful.
Make us one again.

We look to tomorrow,
guided by God's wisdom,
which will cleanse us,
purify and protect us all
in the days ahead.

The Now and the Unknown

Today I ricochet between peace
and every new moment.
Now is the time to start over,
reinvent myself,
begin again.
To once again believe,
as if for the first time,
to pick up where I left off
and start over.
Now is the time to hope,
pray and reimagine
what could be,
to once again
enter the house of the unexpected,
here between chaos and creation,
to engage the unknown future.

The Hovering Presence of Death

Death, where is your sting?
Your hovering presence of fear
echoes in the darkness
of unresolved tomorrows.

May each darkening moment
descend into unknown frontiers
and rise once again
on each new morning.

Harmonized by the rhythms
of each upstart spring of life,
may I dream again
of the beyondness of this moment.

May I stand upright and pay attention
to the events of each passing day.
Yes, today is a burning time.
Fasten your seatbelt, let the fire burn.

Wisdom Time

Thoughts on aging
tumble through my mind.
According to a popular saying,
"Old age is not for sissies."
I wonder what lessons
I am meant to learn
about old age, pain of loss,
lack of confidence,
and even despair.

The aging process
is subtle and sublime.
Sometimes I feel like
I will live forever.
Then a calamity happens
and I feel I'm on the edge
of nothingness,
lost in endless time.
So today I ask,
what is still
possible for me to do?

On a Sunlit Morning

On this sunlit morning
deep down inside
is a dark place, a precipice,
from which I am afraid to fall
and sink into holy mystery.

This precipice of new beginnings
is a place of no return,
at the edge of consciousness,
a sacred place without boundaries,
where I dare to discover my soul.

Walking the Trail

Today is a deep and defining time.
As I walk on the Cosmic Trail
here at Springbank Retreat,
I plunge into my inmost self.

Daisies blooming along the trail
provide a fresh burst of beauty.
Their beauty blows into me
a fresh cosmic force of aliveness.

Leave Something Behind

I want to be remembered,
but not for what I've done
or failed to do.
Do I have a legacy
or is it too late?

Now is the time
to sink solemnly
into the back pages of my life,
to allow hopes and regrets
to dissolve and float away.

The grandfather clock
on the wall reminds me
of the passing of days,
days filled with gratitude.
It is never too late.

Each Breaking Heart

Caskets for children
line roadsides today.
Preparing for burial,
brokenhearted parents
pray their goodbyes.

Thousands of miles away
in Ukraine, war continues to churn.
Children's goodbyes
wash across the fog of war.

Today we gather to pray,
"Bring peace to our world.
May peace descend on our planet
and on each breaking heart."

The Circumference of My Soul

There is a tug at my heart
that wants to live,
an unexpressed impulse
that hovers on the surface
and rises above
the circumference of my soul.

Here, at this intersection
of love and letting go,
I ask: What am I taking with me?
What am I leaving behind?
How do I anticipate
a future replenished with hope?

At Home in the Forest

Embrace the silent forest.
Welcome gurgles of gratitude.
You are at home now.
Enjoy, listen and pray.
You are among the trees,
at home in the forest.

Unity Prayer

As we unite in this sacred moment,
may we be enveloped in ancient wisdom.
In this deep and endless space,
may we find serenity, a time of peace.
May we be held in holy mystery.
May we forge a deep and ever-deepening
bond of love, safety and compassion.
May we knit together our tattered sleeves
and celebrate our capacity to care
for ourselves, our community, our Earth.
Amen.

Panentheism

The notion of panentheism is of great comfort to me.

I often refer to Mechtild of Magdeburg, a German medieval Christian mystic, who said, "The day of my spiritual awakening was the day I saw—and knew I saw—all things in God and God in all things."

The very idea that divinity is infused into the world is a very significant understanding in my life. For me, today, God is not an object or a noun but rather a verb.

Thomas Berry said it best for me when he declared that the divine is a being you cannot feel, see, touch, or smell and is fully present in everything you can.

This is a deep and profound incarnational theology. It announces that God is fully present in life. As some would say, everything is soaked in God.

The Urgency of Geo-Justice

During a staff meeting at Holy Names University, I received a vision that contained the process and possibility of a preferential option for the days ahead. The name that came from this vision revealed the wisdom necessary to define my journey into the challenges of the future.

I called this process geo-justice.

As words bubbled up, I began to give expression to what surfaced in my awareness. I have continued to find expression in and through my heart and life.

As my vision unfolded, I gave expression to this search with the following words: "A personal and planetary challenge, a new context for theological reflection through which we can discover the most urgent tasks that await us on our journey."

I now understand geo-justice from the encyclical of Pope Francis, *Laudato Si': On Care for Our Common Home*. In it, Pope Francis created for the first time in the Catholic tradition the language for a wholistic spirituality. He issued a visionary call to aliveness through passionate and practical action for a deeper understanding of the mysterious journey that unites social and ecological issues.

As I continued to reflect on this process, I experienced a growing sense of urgency. The dynamic synthesis of social and ecological concerns pleads with us to be instruments of beauty and wonder in the world—culminating in what I wish to call a planetary Pentecost.

In and through each defining moment of human-Earth history, we awaken to the experience of a radiant cosmic energy and give great thanks for the manifestation of this moment. Each moment is a celebration and a hope-filled expression of gratitude as we welcome the children of life and respond cheerfully to the silent call of humanity to create a planetary peace in the beauty of the moment that awaits us.

Planetary Pentecost

O how I long to receive
the gift of speaking in tongues,
to be understood
and to understand the gift of oneness.

It will be a defining moment
when I receive the gift, the capacity,
to speak a unifying language
that heals all alienation, all separation, all judgment.

In this new time,
we will no longer experience distance,
obstacles, isolation or loneliness.
We will express and experience
the gifts of each person,
a hope-filled moment of wonder and belonging.

We will be welcomed and supported
in this fresh Pentecostal moment
in which all intuition and imaginings
are nourished and embraced.

In this new time, as if for the first time,
we will speak one language
as we face an unknown future,
immersed in the swirling depths
of a planetary Pentecost.

When Something Happens

Poetry is something that happens
when you feel deeply
and express the meaning of life.
It the awakening of your imagination,
as words bubble up
and speak for themselves,
to heal what seems broken.
Feeling empowered,
you speak with clarity and focus,
as if for the first time.
Yet, some call it confusion,
and others call it prose.
I call it the sacred moment,
because poetic words take you
to other modes of understanding.

Oneness

May we realize,
that even in the midst of differences,
we can feel the overwhelming,
unifying impulse of oneness,
where sacred dimensions
bring us together
and dissolve all jagged edges.
May we embrace
a world of oneness
that allows us to flourish and survive.
May we announce,
awash in rivers of hope,
that we are immersed
in an experience of oneness
that will make us whole again.

Prayer Is About

Prayer happens when we are able to elevate our awareness and go beyond conscious thought.

Prayer is not as much about asking as it is about saying thanks for what is and for what will be.

Prayer is not about give and forgive; it is about gratitude and praise.

Prayer is about the inhalation and exultation of existence.

Prayer is an experience that heals all separation.

Prayer is about the transformation of consciousness.

Prayer is about hope and acts of adoration. Prayer is about caring.

Prayer is about becoming enveloped in the mind and heart of the infinite One who accompanies us through our days.

Prayer is about being immersed in the recesses of life. It is about growing our soul.

Prayer is about paying attention.

Prayer is about "falling down in the grass," according to the guidance of Mary Oliver, whereby we become one with Earth.

Prayer is something we are called to do every day. It is about sinking deeply into every moment of experience, about reading the signs of the times, about deeply imbibing each defining moment in our human-Earth experience.

Prayer is a response to what is going on in the world. It is our capacity to understand each defining moment.

Prayer is about our capacity to flow with the ripples of existence, the pulsations of each new day.

Returning to My Roots

I have unexpectedly rediscovered some of the sources of deep wisdom I originally discovered in my early years. Those years of reading, teaching, and writing about people and programs captured my imagination at the time and engaged my energy. They called me forth into the life I longed for and that I continue to live to this day.

Now when I choose a book by a favorite author, my selection is guided by the conviction that their work reflects the roots of my tradition. The early books by Saul Alinsky remind me of when I was a student in Chicago at the Industrial Area Foundation Training Institute. Reading his books *Reveille for Radicals* and *Rules for Radicals* helps me recall my early years in Chicago as a student in community organization.

Alinsky's work centered on empowerment of the poor and powerless who lived in urban settings. I recall hearing him described as a "therapist to the apathetic." Much of my own writing has focused on global leaders who provide seminal insights into Alinsky's early wisdom. They reactivate my impulse to be engaged in work that can liberate the people and the planet.

I also find myself returning to the prophetic work of Paulo Freire, author of the *Pedagogy of the Oppressed*. As I reread his work, I experience a reactivation of my interest and a renewed commitment to take up the challenge and move forward from whatever holds me back. The work of Freire challenges me to engage in acts of liberation.

The legacies of Alinsky and Freire pulsated in the civil rights movement led by Dr. Martin Luther King, Jr. They also found expression in my attempt to develop programs in geo-justice and engaged cosmology. I remain confident that, prompted by the wisdom of people such as Alinsky and Freire, we will be able to expand our awareness into a time of enhanced harmony, balance, and peace.

Mysticism

Mysticism is a right-brain experience. It is an imaginative experience that activates our creative thinking and summons us to life. To be a mystic is to heal all separation, all exclusively rational thought.

The mystic prays more through the imagination than through the intellect. Prayer becomes an expression of surprise, creativity, and holy wisdom. In our mystical prayers, we become one with the painting, the poem, the puppy, the tree.

We reimagine what it means to be fully alive and awake to each amazing mystery. We listen to what is not yet but remains open in our lives.

Storytelling

Stories of ancestors and prophetic people alter our consciousness and inspire the spirit.

Through stories, we discover our origins in the context of our lives.

In storytelling, the passions of our heart become incarnate through form, figure, and word.

Stories name our relationships and make possible intimacy, love, and celebration.

Stories invite forgiveness and dissolve projection, illusion, and false hope.

In storytelling, we find our voice and discover our identity.

Stories call us to justice-making that is tactile and passionate, igniting the flame of compassion and hope.

Stories are "shamans of the soul." Through stories, we know where we've been, where we are, and where we're going.

Stories of the universe and our own stories find their beginning in the heart of the universe.

Stories enhance our capacity to perceive how the patterns of our lives reveal a greater purpose.

Stories illuminate the moment.

Stories foster reciprocity and animate circles of wisdom and concern.

Sacred Impulse

The sacred impulse challenges us to develop networks of security and trust, new constellations of relationship that hold out the promise of profound integration as we soften the boundaries between intimacy and contemplation, feminine and masculine, action and reflection, and as we move forward with hope into a time of unprecedented harmony, balance, and peace.

The sacred impulse is an inclination to act, a preoccupation that prompts us to respond—a nagging feeling, a hunch, an unplanned magnetic intuition, a movement from the inside out, an awareness of spirit that hovers over the cosmos and summons us to life.

The sacred impulse ignites the fire of our imaginations and the stirrings of the heart.

The sacred impulse is an eruption of the pulsating energy of God that calls us to love and compassion through the heart and fire of the cosmos and our lives.

The sacred impulse invites us to leave behind a worldview that is forced, static, and stuck.

A Poet's Impulse

This morning I feel alive,
filled with wonder,
awaiting a surprise.
Is this not the day
when the cosmos will burst
into words of wonder and amazement,
when something unprecedented will happen,
when tender hearts will be born
with a poet's impulse?

Images

My imagination is filled with wonder, engagement, and surprise as I take up the challenge to prepare for a sacred new tomorrow.

Sacred images trickle into my awareness and flow with the possibilities of all that awaits us and all that needs to be done.

Our challenge today is to become liberated from the patterns of the past and to imagine a future shaped and formed by each moment of the unexpected.

I visualize and pray that a world of emerging possibilities may be evoked in each of us, an era in which we can be totally alive and prompted by acts of oneness.

As we engage as both mystics and prophets, may we become threshold people, moving forward soaked in sacred moments of creativity and compassion.

Each day, we awaken from the tranquilized obviousness embedded in the dominant culture. We invoke breakthroughs prompted by a listening heart.

May we march forward into the future, convinced that God is alive and at our side.

As we anticipate the future, we gratefully and hopefully feel that tomorrow will turn out well.

As we soar into the future, may we become increasingly aware that we are powered by the spirit in this fresh and liberating moment. May we heal all separation and be propelled by the power of paradox.

Each of us is empowered by the vision of Archimedes, who long ago proclaimed, "If you give me a lever and a place to stand, I can move the world."

If we deal with our anger, we can find the courage and wisdom needed to become a people of the future, a people empowered to move the world, to make a difference and heal the broken heart of our endangered planet.

People who live on the margins are often at the center of what needs to be done.

May we venture forth, energized and supported for the future.

Like Dr. Martin Luther King, Jr., may all of us be inspired by a dream.

Like Nina Simone, may we discover what it means to be free.

Like Jesus of Nazareth, may we transform the world.

And with the wisdom of Thomas Berry, may we envision a future better than all the past.

Prompted by the flourishing beauty of Earth and the need for healing of our planet, may we look forward to doing whatever needs to be done—personally and planetary-wise.

Amen.

Activating the Impulse

Life consistently presents us with challenges and change. One such challenge occurs when, through a sacred impulse, we begin to see the world differently and live out the implications of the new creation story.

Through childhood memories, we experience again the grandeur of creation and the beauty, power, mystery, and majesty of life.

We experience a deep mystical unity and know again the exaltation of existence.

We are rescued from a world of online shopping malls and consumer relationships.

We experience again the flora and fauna of our childhood home—the rivers, strawberries, thunderstorms, and boats, the many faces of creation.

At its deepest level, creativity is living out the paschal event; we live and die to our mortality and rise to make a contribution that will live on after us.

The creative process confronts us with the forces of life, death, and rebirth. At its heart, the creative process is an impulse toward immortality—reaching for a way to give birth to a project, idea, or child.

We are initiated into a vital relationship with the divine. The imagination erupts, the spirit stirs, the heart opens, and wisdom occurs in the recesses of our souls. Our path unfolds, and we discover through self-expression intimacy with the divine, with humanity, and with the other-than-human world.

The natural world is our introduction into a living relationship with the divine, through which we discover destiny, joy, and fulfillment.

When we listen to the poor, the neglected child, the abused wife, the forsaken tree, or the polluted beach, our awareness expands and we feel closer to God.

When we listen to the voiceless, our energy increases and we understand in new ways that the transformation of the planet is a spiritual task.

When we are receptive to the voice of the poor, we experience sacredness and are more present to what really matters.

Discover Yourself in the Great Unfolding

We live within a dynamic unfolding cosmos.

Each day, we continue our search for meaning, as fresh insights and emergent understandings come into our mind.

Each day, we are astonished as amazing new understandings tumble into our awareness.

Moment by moment, we celebrate a continuous unfolding of discovery as our search moves into each evolutionary moment.

Each day, we realize that we are sinking into a new phase of consciousness, a time that is both cosmic and uniquely our own.

In and through this, we plunge into new forms of awareness. We imagine a fresh, ultimate wisdom, a powerful process that is charged with value and beauty.

Each day, we envision our calling to be engaged in the great work of our time, to build a cathedral for friends and companions who call out, to heal what is broken.

In this great unfolding, may whatever is torn and tattered in you be healed.

We live within a dynamic cosmos.
Each day, we continue our search for meaning.
Fresh insights and amazing understandings
tumble into our awareness.
We celebrate each evolutionary moment
as we sink into a new consciousness
that is both cosmic and uniquely our own.
In and through this plunge,
we imagine a powerful process
charged with value and beauty.
We follow our calling into the great work,
as architects of a new cultural synthesis,
working together to build a cathedral,
a holistic and imaginative community,
each of us discovering ourselves
as the universe unfolds.

Cosmic People

As we navigate the transition from cosmos to cosmogenesis, all distance, all separation, and all dualism are healed. We visualize and reimagine that the small self is united once again with the great self. We watch as paradox happens and healing takes place. At this moment, we become truly cosmic people, with a truly global view. We are nourished by the ancestral grace of the past and we remain open to the surprise of the future. In this way, a deep cosmic genetic community can be born.

The Impulse That Affirms

We let go of a worldview
that desacralizes life,
denigrates the intellect,
represses spontaneity,
denies death,
devalues story, creativity, sacredness, the poor,
and then blames the prophets
and teachers of today.
The sacred impulse
celebrates our epic of existence
and summons us
to insight and intimacy
as we embrace more fully
the heart and fire
of our planetary journey.
The impulse that affirms
is the impulse of the spirit
that gives us breath and life.

Longing I Hope You Will Hear

There is an ache in my heart
that yearns to live,
a hunger in my soul
that wants to thrive.
On this frosty winter morning,
here at the edge of my longing,
I reflect on the meaning of life.
I ponder what's next.
The joys and sorrows,
hopes and dreams,
hovering my heart
cry out to be recognized.
Please listen. I hope you will hear.

The Call to Our Great Work

Today I feel grateful and enveloped by the comfort of my soul. For the first time, I feel focused on the needs of the world and what I'm called to do. Thomas Berry, among others, had a name for this. He called it the *great work*. With this vision in mind, we become empowered to move into the future with a fresh focus and purpose. Our call to the great work is an invitation to embark on whatever needs to be done.

At this sacred moment in human-Earth history, our focus on the great work liberates us from the imprisonment in a culture of vocationalism. We take up the challenge to engage in the fulfillment of our destiny.

The great work can be understood as a response to the signs of the times. It is a response to the joys and sorrows of the people and the Earth. Through this response, we are able to fulfill our original purpose. May we join with colleagues and friends to compose a new chapter in our journey and shared dream experience.

The Call to Here and Now

I increasingly see
the wisdom of paradox
revealed moment by moment
in the apparent contradictions of life.

The wisdom in each moment
dances between the eternal truths
and the new beginnings
revealed in the dynamic intuition
in the here and now of life.

Terminal Phase

What does one do
in the terminal phase of life,
when one feels overwhelmed
by sorrow, lost energy,
things yet to be accomplished?
How does one come to terms with endings,
with regret for all the illusions one created
about what one thought
one should accomplish?

God, Where Are You?

Are You in the forest or the trees?
Are You glistening in the morning sun
or on the street where addicts live,
crying out for more intoxicants
to be numbed each dark and dingy night?
Are You with the children frolicking
in the soft green fields
or are You in the killing fields of war
and gun-infested cities of this land?

God, where are You?

Are You with the people
gathered on the arid land
where hungry souls thirst for joy each sunlit day?
Are You among the unhoused
crying out for shelter tonight?
Or are You here in the longing hearts
of all who cherish the beauty of this day?
Are You in the sacred silent moment
that welcomes solitude each new morning?

God, where are You?

Are You gathered with friends
whose companions call out
for the healing of each tattered soul?

O Sacred One of sacred days,
as we heal from anger,
we invoke courage and are grateful
that You are with us now.
You are here today and
You bring us hope.

Poetry Journey

Some would say
poetry takes us into a time
when we have nothing to say.
Yet here you are, saying it.
May this be a day
when your imagination awakens
to gather energy and heal what is broken.
As words flow across the page,
they take us to other modes of understanding.
We call it poetry.

Working With Matthew Fox

I was fortunate to have met Matthew and to have been his student at a time when I was struggling to make connections between my own background and what I had learned about social justice. Inspired by Matt's vision of creation-centered spirituality, I began to write and teach at Holy Names University. The emphasis of our curriculum was on culture, psychology, and justice. One night after a faculty meeting, I had a dream that we should name the justice part of our program "Geo-Justice." Since that time, geo-justice has been a primary focus of my teaching and writing.

Matt, along with Leonardo Buff and others, encountered resistance from the Church hierarchy. As a result, Leonardo ceased to be a member of the Franciscan order, and Matt chose to become an Anglican priest. Matt said he didn't want to "lose his driver's license." By that, he meant he wanted to continue to function as a priest.

To be fully honest and transparent, I contributed in some ways to that difficult time. I felt caught between the wishes of the University's administration and the vision of Matt's work. Today, all these years later, I want to publicly apologize for anything I did that contributed to the oppression of his work.

I want to emphasize my gratitude for Matt's influence in my life. I want to do whatever I can to reignite our common interests and to support his ongoing prophetic work.

Memories and Reflections:
Brian Thomas Swimme

I first met Brian in the summer of 1983.

I met him at Matthew Fox's home, with other members of the staff of the Institute in Culture and Creation Spirituality (ICCS). My intention was to come to California for a conversation to see whether it would be an appropriate place to do my sabbatical in the fall. Shortly after my arrival, Brian and Matt excused themselves, as they were offering a weekend at the Esalen Institute.

Early in the semester, I attended Brian's class on the new cosmology. One evening, during the break, I spoke to Brian. I had studied metaphysics and theology during my seminary days, and I told Brian that in my understanding, he was the metaphysician of the program there.

His book *The Universe Is a Green Dragon* was published that year, 1984. It remains a marvelous and accessible story on the new cosmology.

Brian also taught a class called "The Artist as Spiritual Voyager." He grounded it in the work developed by Dante and revealed the creation-centered dimension of the ICCS program, which focused on creativity, ecology, and justice. I took this class, and so did his wife, Denise.

When Matthew Fox left ICCS, I turned to Brian for support. He and other remaining faculty met to re-envision the program. We were also guided by faculty member Dorothy Donneley.

Following his years of teaching at Holy Names, Brian accepted an invitation from the president of the California Institute of Integral Studies (CIIS) to join their faculty. Even so, he continued to teach in my class one day each semester as well as to participate in the summer institutes that were held at Holy Names, under the auspices of the Sophia Center. Brian was the keynote speaker for these events, which brought people from around the country and beyond to address such themes as global prophets and which focused on the work of Teilhard de Chardin, Thomas Berry, Rosemary Reuther, and many others.

During his time teaching at CIIS, which continues to this day, Brian created many programs and innovative books. Following publication of *Journey of the Universe*, coauthored with Mary Evelyn Tucker of Yale University, a film by the same name was produced and seen around the world, with Brian as the commentator. In *The Hidden Heart of the Cosmos*, Brian included graphics to illustrate his thoughts. He was proud that those graphics were produced by his son.

Each semester, our class at Springbank takes the opportunity to view a sample of Brian's work. Of particular interest to our participants is his video *The Powers of the Universe*. Brian's doctorate was in gravitational physics, and he writes about the twelve intercorrelated cosmological powers. The third power, *allurement,* is a spiritual, cosmic analogy for gravitational physics.

Currently, Brian has been working on a developing understanding of Teilhard's work based on the theme of the noosphere. In this focus, we are able to comprehend how the universe is unfolding and in a sense discover and celebrate a new story in the great unfolding.

At this time, Brian teaches part time at CIIS, while at the same time leading a program called The Human Energy Project, which is an innovative continuation of his work.

Brian's most recent book is *Cosmogenesis*. This important work marks a defining moment in our journey with the universe. The challenge and questions Brian poses are an invitation to each of us. May you take to heart and experience the cosmogenesis of this moment.

Photo: Brian Thomas Swimme

Reproductive Imagination

Together we set out to engage in a profound transformation of humanity. This transformation can begin through the practice of reproductive imagination. *Reproductive imagination* simply means the capacity to recall past events. It is significant because, if humans can recall past events, we can then reflect on them. And if we reflect on them, we can also respond to them in the present moment. Humans have not always possessed or fully used this capacity.

We can use our imagination to transform our consciousness, as we listen deeply to the universe story. We can recall the contributions of global prophets, such as Thomas Berry, Matthew Fox, Brian Thomas Swimme, Ilia Delio, and others. And we can recall the defining moments in our lives that have shaped and formed our cosmic journey.

We can venture into a new level of talent and a new telling and a new understanding of the divine and of ourselves. We can unfold into a precious, sacred moment of creativity and change.

An Explosion of Wisdom

As we shift from cosmos to cosmogenesis, all distance and separation are healed. We reimagine the relationship of the small self with the great Self.

Today and every day is the time to reactivate our imaginations, to realize who we are and who we're meant to be.

We are all global people, with the hunger and wisdom to expand beyond our smallness.

As we wander into the future, may we arrive at a new amazing place. May we become more fully alive, more fully open to the surprise knocking on our doorstep.

Today I ask, "How did it all begin?" Was it not a vast explosion that cascaded from hydrogen to oxygen?

Something amazing happened; the cosmos was filled with oceans of grace. Wondrous swells of energy spread awareness across a cosmic-colored sky. I stand in radical amazement, aware that a marvelous promise is about to be born.

And so I ask, "Why am I here?" Who are we as we arrive in this manger of surprise?

Something new is happening; something not previously perceived is flowing into life. Yes, we are in the manger, the birth place of the unexpected.

We feel the urgency to pray into new ways of seeing.

Today I realize why I'm here, why I was born, how I can contribute to my purpose and my great work.

I was born into the world to discover this secret place of holy mystery.

A master narrative is being told, moment by moment, by artists, poets, musicians, and meditation leaders, along with every flower, puppy, tree, and moment of sunshine. Every storyteller who breaks into voice alerts us in this time of sacred silence. As we witness and anticipate this emergent story of an even more mutually enhancing and hope-filled sacred moment, we give expression to the deepest creativity in the universe.

As I journey into the forest of wisdom, I invite you to join me, to listen to the guidance of the vast universe and discover and celebrate your life purpose.

A Poem on Earth

Earth is still and sunny
on this December day.
Shelly lounges in the yard,
enjoys the sunshine
on this Advent afternoon.
Today the love of God and friends
takes on deeper meaning
as I welcome the Bethlehems of life.
In the manger of my heart,
I wait and pray and ask:
What will be born on Earth today?
What will be born in us tomorrow?

A Merton Moment

He built a bridge between our hearts and life,
taught us how to live with a satisfied mind.
He showed us a new moment of transparency
and how to remember the good times.
He called us forth to rejoice in life
and discover gratitude for silence.
He wanted us to be deeply engaged
in moments of beauty and healing.
We could say he was both a poet and a politician.
More than once, he fell in love
as he encountered silence and friends,
as isolation ceased and imagination returned.

Farewell, Holy Names

Holy Names University is closing its doors in 2023.

I spent thirty-one years at HNU. I arrived in the late summer of 1984, in time for the fall semester. It was to be my fall sabbatical leave. But I stayed for many years more.

A community of women from Quebec, Canada, founded Holy Names in 1868. In the twentieth century, many HNU students were the first generation in their families to receive a higher education.

Memories flood my mind. Here are just a handful.

Sr. Delores Rashford and I worked together on a committee to ensure that the spirituality program was in line with the regulations of the University. Sr. Delores passed away recently.

Sr. Francesca Cabrini Weber's gifts of humor remain with me when I recall our Christmas parties during those days. She served as graduate dean.

Sr. Deborah Church was an international scholar and historian.

Sr. Carol Selman's music filled the chapel on special occasions. She has served as vice president for mission fulfillment from the past up to today.

Also deeply held in my memory are the many students who received their master's degrees in culture and creation spirituality when I was a member of the HNU faculty.

I pray that HNU's legacy will live on in the hearts and minds of all who remember this sacred institution.

Come to Springbank

The people who come to Springbank
are generous, talented, open-hearted.
They are people of goodness,
of vision and hope.

Prompted by an impulse,
a guiding star that provides context,
they come here wondering
what's next in their life.

And they come with conviction
that what they dream of
can still happen,
the fulfillment of their wildest dreams.

New Beginnings

The sun is up.
Shelly has had breakfast,
we have gone for a walk.
May it be a day
of new beginnings
for each of us, I pray.
May it be a time
to make the great transition,
to give thanks for what has happened
and then begin again
Today I pray,
may the gospel of our people
bring us hope.
So may it be, O creator God.
Amen.

Hymns From the Hermitage

I sit here in the hermitage
at Springbank Retreat.
On this cold December day,
I listen to the music in my heart.

I am not alone today.
I feel the vitality of love,
surrounded as I am by
a celestial choir of singers.

I ask them what their lives are about.
Their generous and wise reply is
"You have to make people laugh
and you have to make them cry."

My Story in Pictures

Throughout the years
I have welcomed you to the Pine Hermitage,
which I now call my home.
On the walls of this building,
I have photos of family and friends.
Each is a chapter of new beginnings.
Each is a reminder of the past
and a promise of tomorrow.
Among the pictures
are my mother and father, sister and brother,
as they recline on the shores of Lake Huron,
just a few miles from where I was born.
Also included are my classmates
from Wallaceburg District High School.
And my degrees from
Assumption University of Windsor
and St. Peter's Seminary in London, Ontario.
Among others, these pictures tell my story.

Behind Locked Doors

Today I ask what's next in my life.
The answer that comes back
is another question:
"Is there an answer?"

Probably not.
It seems the answer
is written in foreign words
behind locked doors.

Perhaps it's time to pause
the questions hidden in my heart,
and instead respond to Mary Oliver,
who asked, "What is it you plan to do
with your one wild and precious life?"

And so I looked to the future
with relentless enthusiasm
for the not-yet and
for whatever will come my way.

Winter Solstice at Springbank

On this rain-soaked morning,
we gaze into silence,
wonder about solstice,
about the meaning of
this shortest day of the year.
On this cold December morning,
we wonder and wait
for the sun to return.
On this dark day, I pray
to learn the lesson of solstice.
May this celebration of absence
fill the longing in my heart.

Reinvention

How do you reinvent yourself,
become new again,
transcend boundaries,
descend into the depths
and once more start over?

You are invited to heal
all separation, all dualism,
to come home to yourself
and take up the challenges
of everyday life.

As awareness infuses
you with insight and energy,
become new again,
alive to the radiant flow
of each dimension of existence.

Through the surge of cosmic energy,
you are called forth to reinvent yourself.
And become one again,
in and through this moment,
as you enter a defining opportunity
in human-Earth history.

This Is Where You Belong

We are at a crossroads
at a time of endings and new beginnings,
at the invocation of a moment
that is not yet and is about to be.
We gather with every fragment of newness,
every molecule of wonder, wish and surprise.
Here at the intersection,
we dare to announce
both what is and what is to be.

Today, something new is being born,
a promise for tomorrow
and a deeply felt gratitude for what is to come.
I give thanks and wonder
and pray the great amens of our tradition,
whose imprint and accomplishments
are alive, flourishing and entirely new.

Today, we welcome each child of the universe.
Each of us in our community of life, Earth and spirit
is being born anew.
This is who you are
and this is what you're called to discover.
Welcome to your sacred fragile home.
This is where you belong.

Everybody Waved

It's early today, breakfast is over.
Friends prepare for departure—
some to Kentucky, others to Dublin
and across the land.

Eventually everyone leaves.
I think of the film produced in Canada
many, many years ago.
It was called *Nobody Waves Goodbye.*

Today it is a different moment
here at Springbank.
I am changing the title to
Everybody Waved Goodbye.

Epilogue: Concluding Prayer

As we prepare for our departure
and anticipate the future,
we spend a few moments to reflect on
our insights, learning
and enhanced sensitivity to Earth's beauty
flourishing here at Springbank.

We understand that the story of the universe
is not contained in a book
but is an event taking place all around us.
We anticipate a future
filled with gratitude and
sprinkled with seasons of hope.

About the Author

Jim Conlon was born in Canada in 1936. He received a degree in chemistry from Assumption University of Windsor, and later in theology from the University of Western Ontario, and a PhD from Union Institute and University. Deeply moved by the impact of the second Vatican Council, the civil rights movement, and the Vietnam War, Jim moved from pastoral work to the streets. He was the recipient of the 2013 Thomas Berry Award.

For more information and a complete list of Jim's published works, see: www.jimconlon.net.

Contact: Springbank: 843-372-6311 or
        springbank@springbankretreat.org

www.ingramcontent.com/pod-product-compliance
Lightning Source LLC
Chambersburg PA
CBHW051525120626
46551CB00012B/1077